IT'S TIME TO EAT RICE

It's Time to Eat
RICE

Walter the Educator

Silent King Books
A WhichHead Entertainment Imprint

Copyright © 2024 by Walter the Educator

All rights reserved. No part of this book may be reproduced in any manner whatsoever without written per- mission except in the case of brief quotations embodied in critical articles and reviews.

First Printing, 2024

Disclaimer

This book is a literary work; the story is not about specific persons, locations, situations, and/or circumstances unless mentioned in a historical context. Any resemblance to real persons, locations, situations, and/or circumstances is coincidental. This book is for entertainment and informational purposes only. The author and publisher offer this information without warranties expressed or implied. No matter the grounds, neither the author nor the publisher will be accountable for any losses, injuries, or other damages caused by the reader's use of this book. The use of this book acknowledges an understanding and acceptance of this disclaimer.

It's Time to Eat RICE is a collectible early learning book by Walter the Educator suitable for all ages belonging to Walter the Educator's Time to Eat Book Series. Collect more books at WaltertheEducator.com

USE THE EXTRA SPACE TO TAKE NOTES AND DOCUMENT YOUR MEMORIES

RICE

It's time to eat rice, so soft and so white,

It's Time to Eat

Rice

A bowl full of goodness, a pure delight.

Fluffy and warm, it's ready to share,

Rice is a dish that's beyond compare!

You can eat it plain, so simple and sweet,

Or mix it with veggies for a savory treat.

Add beans or chicken, or fish from the sea,

Rice goes with everything, just wait and see!

Fried rice is tasty, with eggs and peas,

Cooked in a pan with a little breeze.

It sizzles and pops, so golden and fine,

Every bite is a flavor divine!

Brown rice is nutty, with a hearty taste,

It's healthy and filling, no need to waste.

With soup or curry, or wrapped in a roll,

Rice is a food that makes you feel whole.

It's Time to Eat

Rice

Sticky rice clumps, so fun to hold,

Perfect with mango or wrapped in gold.

In sushi it shines, so neat and small,

Rice makes the meal the best of them all!

Jasmine rice smells like a sweet perfume,

It fills up the air and brightens the room.

Basmati is long, so fluffy and light,

Each grain is a star, shining so bright!

Rice is a traveler, it's been everywhere,

From faraway lands to tables we share.

It grows in paddies with water and sun,

A gift from the earth for everyone.

Cooking rice is easy, just add some heat,

Watch it puff up, so soft and neat.

Steam it or boil it, there's no wrong way,

It's Time to Eat

Rice

Rice is a friend you'll love every day!

So grab your spoon, it's time to begin,

Scoop up the rice and let the fun in.

Whether it's plain or spiced up so nice,

Nothing's as wonderful as eating rice!

Let's cheer for rice, both near and far,

The best little grains, a food superstar!

Say it together, with smiles so wide,

It's Time to Eat

Rice

"Hooray for rice, our mealtime pride!"

ABOUT THE CREATOR

Walter the Educator is one of the pseudonyms for Walter Anderson. Formally educated in Chemistry, Business, and Education, he is an educator, an author, a diverse entrepreneur, and he is the son of a disabled war veteran. "Walter the Educator" shares his time between educating and creating. He holds interests and owns several creative projects that entertain, enlighten, enhance, and educate, hoping to inspire and motivate you. Follow, find new works, and stay up to date with Walter the Educator™ at WaltertheEducator.com

www.ingramcontent.com/pod-product-compliance
Lightning Source LLC
LaVergne TN
LVHW012052070526
838201LV00082B/4034